Dare to Be...

A series of inspiring and uplifting poems for children. Life lessons for young people, from tots to teens.

Kendra L. Kaufman

Illustrated by Ana F. Stone

ISBN 978-1-64559-210-5 (Paperback)
ISBN 978-1-64559-211-2 (Digital)

Copyright © 2019 Kendra L. Kaufman
All rights reserved
First Edition

All rights reserved. No part of this publication may be reproduced, distributed, or transmitted in any form or by any means, including photocopying, recording, or other electronic or mechanical methods without the prior written permission of the publisher. For permission requests, solicit the publisher via the address below.

Covenant Books, Inc.
11661 Hwy 707
Murrells Inlet, SC 29576
www.covenantbooks.com

For Riley

Your Heavenly Father loves you. He created you to be unique and has a special purpose for your life. I pray that as you grow, you come to know Him personally and discover all the wonderful blessings He has for you.

Contents

Different 2
Loud 3
Honest 6
Imaginative 7
Faithful 10
Silly 11
Excellent 14
Loving 15
Neat 17
Polite 20
Obedient 21
Unpopular 23
Alone 26
Busy 27
Humble 30
Forgiving 31
Healthy 34
Smart 35
Responsible 38
You 39

Different

Some people are tall. Some people are short.
Some are athletic and they play a sport.

Some people wear glasses. Some people wear braces.
While others are funny—they make silly faces.

People are born with hair black, blond, or brown.
Sometimes it sticks up. Sometimes it lays down.

Maybe you have locks that are fiery red.
Perhaps you haven't any hair on top of your head!

It doesn't matter—the color of your eyes, hair, or skin.
Whether you're tall or short; if you're stocky or thin…

Whether your teeth are crooked or straight as a line,
you are the product of God's perfect design.

God made us all different—thank goodness for that!
Wouldn't it be boring if we all shared one hat?

Dare to be different—there's no one like you!
Be proud of yourself, and love yourself too!

Loud

There are times to be quiet. You know those times well.
At church, in the library, or after the bell...

But there are times to be loud, when your voice must be heard.
You have to roar like a lion, not chirp like a bird.

When your favorite team is winning—that's a good time to cheer!
Clap your hands and shout! Let everyone hear!

When you see something wrong, that's not the time to be still.
Stand up for what's right. Be one of strong will.

Stand up to bullies. Tell them they're wrong.
Don't laugh with approval and don't play along.

Doing the right thing won't make you popular with the crowd.
But it's foolish to join in mischief and do what's not allowed.

Take a stand against evil. If you see it, use your voice!
You'll sleep well at night, knowing you made a Godly choice!

Honest

Accidents happen—to me and to you.
But parents know well when our stories aren't true.

If glasses get broken or tubs overflow,
lying won't help—they already know.

Just say you're sorry. It goes a long way.
Mom may still be angry, but here's what she'll say:

"You took responsibility—for that I am glad.
But understand this, it doesn't mean I'm not mad.

Let's clean up this mess, then no more TV.
But if you had lied, think how much worse it would be!"

The consequences given may hurt for a day,
but consider the future, what people will say.

"They're of high moral character, and their words are true!"
What an honor to have others say this of you.

So dare to be honest. You'll command much respect.
People will trust you. You'll have many friends, I suspect.

Imaginative

Keep your eyes open to things that aren't there.
A one-legged pirate or a big grizzly bear.

Defend your castle against a fire-breathing dragon.
Explore the Wild West in your old, covered wagon.

Slide over rainbows. Swing from the stars.
Be the first person to walk upon Mars.

Children are best at imagining things
while adults forget how much happiness it brings.

So keep the magic alive! Always be curious!
Stay young at heart. Don't be so serious!

Faithful

Some days are easy. Some days are hard.
Bad weather will come, so be on your guard.

Even mighty trees are brought low
when clouds become dark and the wind starts to blow.

Although you may feel like you're on your own,
you don't have to go through the storm all alone.

Whenever life's woes have you singing the blues,
be of good cheer; I have some great news!

There's victory in Jesus; the battle has been won!
Praise the name of Jesus, God's one and only Son!

Keep your faith in God. Take the time to pray.
He knows all your troubles. He will make a way.

So stand strong and tall, like the mighty trees of yore.
The storm will soon end. You'll come out stronger than before.

Silly

Silliness is something that helps keep you young.
So scrunch up your nose and wiggle your tongue.

Swing like a monkey. Snort like a pig.
Act like a clown and put on a wig.

Your parents may frown and ask what you're doing
when you bark like a dog or when you start mooing.

"Making you laugh." That's what you should say
when Mom and Dad ask why you're acting this way.

Then they will smile. You've brightened their day
with your animal sounds and child-like play.

Dare to be silly. Laughing is free!
Make people smile. See how fun it can be!

Excellent

None of us are perfect. No, not even you.
No matter how much you'd like to be, you know it's just not true.

But you can be excellent! "What do you mean?" you ask.
Simply pour your whole heart into every single task.

Try your best at everything—schoolwork, sports, or chores.
Your determination and work ethic will open many doors.

There will be obstacles and people who stand in the way of your success.
Keep your head up! Stay determined. Fight your way through that mess.

With hard work and persistence, you'll accomplish a lot.
Write a story, build a house, or be an astronaut.

Aim high! Dream big! Pour your heart into your task.
Set goals. Try your best. That's all anyone could ask.

Loving

We live in a world where it's, "What about me?"
But the Bible tells us that's not how it should be.

Take care of your friends. Help out your brother.
Lend people a hand. Love one another.

It doesn't seem hard. This you can do!
But Jesus had said, "Love your enemies," too!

"How can I do this?" you'll probably ask.
Why were we left with this difficult task?

God wants His people to love pure and true.
"Do unto others as you would have them do unto you" (Lk 6:31, NIV).

Dare to love as God does. Just sit and think this through.
You need to love your fellow man, just as God loves you.

Neat

What's under your bed? Go ahead, take a peek.
You might find the homework that was due this past week.

Candy wrappers, stinky socks,
picture books, wooden blocks.

Used tissues, your old backpack,
a dirty dish from last night's snack.

If you can't see the floor and the hamper overflows,
you're likely to trip and hurt your little toes.

Mom looks at the mess and frowns in disgust
when she sees all the laundry and layers of dust.

It's truly unacceptable; you really must confess,
to not clean your room and live with such a mess.

So take out the trash and vacuum the rugs.
By keeping it clean, you won't invite bugs.

If you don't want creepy-crawlies visiting at night,
keep filth to a minimum. Then you'll be alright.

And what about yourself? Keep yourself clean, too!
Wash your hands. Brush your teeth. Shower with shampoo!

Clean the dirt from your nails. Run a comb through your hair.
Do your laundry as needed; it shows that you care.

If you're looking for a way to live with less stress,
put things away. Clean up that mess!

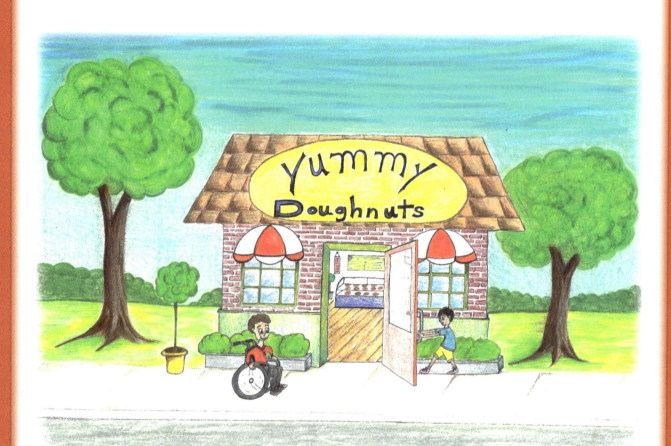

Polite

Common courtesy has become a long lost art.
Since we dropped this tradition, society's come apart.

We used to care for one another, put others before ourselves.
Now there seems to be a war—each man for themselves.

Hold the door for someone else and let them go in first.
Give food to the hungry and water to those who thirst.

Don't use foul language. It's ugly and shows no class.
Be respectful of your elders. Don't give them any sass.

Share your things with those around you. Don't be quick to scold.
Bless others with your kindness. It'll come back a hundred-fold.

Dare to be polite, even if the world seems mean.
Put others' comfort before your own. Don't be a drama queen.

Obedient

The Bible says to honor your mother and father.
There may be times when you ask yourself, "why bother?"

They've been around for a while.
They've experienced a lot.
There's wisdom to be gained from them.
Even if it seems there's not.

If you hear "no," it's for good reason.
They're aware of things you don't understand.
Mom and Dad love you dearly,
but need to keep you well in hand.

If children get their every wish,
they won't appreciate what they own.
They won't know contentment
and they'll be difficult to deal with when grown.

There will be times when you don't agree
with grumpy Mom and Dad.
You'll want your way and then they'll say,
"Oh, gee, that's just too bad."

You may not understand their reasons.
They'll sometimes make you mad.
But to fully honor God,
you must first honor Mom and Dad.

Be content with your parents' decisions
which are made out of love for you.
Mom and Dad are responsible for your safety
and everything you do.

Unpopular

They say, "Clothes make the man." That's so incredibly <u>un</u>true!
It's the things you can't see—it's what's inside of you.

Character. Honesty. Generosity. Respect.
These are the ingredients you need to inject.

If people don't accept you for the person that you are,
they're not worth knowing. Heed this warning. Stay far!

If the popular kids are all bullies and brats,
you'd have better company in a roomful of rats.

They boss people around. They're not good friends at all.
They'll tell you what to do and laugh when you fall.

Making fun of people is wrong. Yet bullies think they're cool.
They'll point and laugh, call people names, and try to run the school.

Surround yourself with people you don't need to impress with your athletic skills or the way that you dress.

Don't try to change the person God made you to be because your Father in heaven says, "You're special to Me."

Alone

Take a deep breath. Don't get yourself stressed.
Silence is golden—let your soul rest.

So turn off the music. Don't make a sound.
Take a deep breath. Peace will be found.

Being alone—it's not a bad thing.
It's a good time for prayer. It's a good time to sing.

Friends are great, but you can do lots on your own.
Go fishing, ride a bike, or play the trombone!

Turn off the gadgets. Instead, read a book!
Color a picture. Help Mom and Dad cook!

There's so much to do! Don't let yourself get bored!
Join the choir of angels. Sing praises to the Lord!

Busy

We all have the same amount of time in a day.
But if spent unwisely, it'll all slip away.

While it may be fun watching hours of TV,
look in the mirror—you may not like what you see.

Some people twiddle their thumbs playing video games;
while others do homework—they have higher aims.

Dare to be busy. Keep your goals in mind.
Don't let your time slip away. Don't get left behind.

Entertainment is fine but not your only reason to live.
You were created for a purpose and have so much to give!

Never stop learning! Always try new things!
Life's surprises await you. Trust the King of Kings!

Your Heavenly Father may not reveal all His perfect plans.
But without Him you can do nothing, so stay in His loving hands.

Humble

Proud folks love to brag. They think they're better than the rest.
They'll take any opportunity to prove why he or she is best.

Proud people demand high honors. They'll feel disrespected
if they don't receive the attention and the praise that they expected.

We are all servants of Jesus Christ. He has no VIPs.
Those with hearts of pomp and pride will be brought to their knees.

Don't be too proud to ask for help and admit when you are wrong.
You're obviously not perfect, don't try to be headstrong.

You should be proud of yourself and have good self-esteem.
But you're not better than anyone else on the team.

All your talents and all your gifts come from God above.
To help further His Kingdom, serve others with selfless love.

Dare to be humble, so when others hear your story—
it will clearly say to them, "To God be ALL the glory!"

Forgiving

Sometimes people hurt our feelings. It can make us sad.
And if they don't apologize, we can get quite mad.

They may call us names, look at us weird, or make us feel left out.
They'll make us want to cry. They'll make us want to shout.

Sometimes people hurt our feelings, even when they don't mean to.
That's because they don't see things through the same eyes that we do.

Forgiving people is a process. It doesn't happen overnight.
Especially if your heartache resulted from a fight.

But as you keep on forgiving, it gets easier each day
to let go of the past until the pain goes away.

If we don't forgive our enemies, we've given them great power
to negatively affect our hearts and cause our moods to sour.

So forgive those that hurt you, whether they apologize or not.
Don't let your heart get hard. Don't let your spirit rot.

Forgiving isn't easy. We like to hold a grudge.
But God cannot forgive us, if we do not budge.

So dare to be forgiving to those who cause you pain.
Let Jesus take your baggage and freedom you will gain!

Healthy

Your body has an engine just like a car.
It turns food into fuel so you can go far.

But if you put bad gas into the tank
the engine will sputter, or it won't crank.

To help keep your body running at its best,
simply be mindful of what you ingest.

While we all like our diets of cookies and chips,
the sugar and carbs go straight to our hips.

Eat the colors of the rainbow. Remember: white is not good.
Get plenty of exercise and rest like you should.

Dare to be healthy. You'll have less aches and pains.
Your body's a temple where the Holy Ghost reigns!

Smart

Libraries used to be popular places
to check out some books and meet some new faces.

When down time was used to strengthen the brain
until today's TV flushed it all down the drain.

The more effort you put into finding a fact,
the more likely it'll make a greater impact.

So if you have a question, don't be quick to ask your phone.
Do a little research and find the answer on your own.

Memorize some basic facts in history, math, and art.
Don't fill your head with lots of junk. Let yourself get smart.

There's so much of history that you ought to learn
that's not in your schoolbooks but is of your concern.

Read some classic literature like Orwell, Dickens, or Twain.
You'll enhance your vocabulary and exercise your brain.

There's so much of the world that's not on your TV,
that's actually a lot more fun. I dare you, go and see!

Responsible

Lazy people make excuses and think they're somehow owed.
But why should they reap the benefits of what they haven't sowed?

You are responsible for your own success. It won't happen overnight.
Be wise in your decision-making and keep your goals in sight.

Weigh your options carefully before choosing a path to take.
Be prepared for the consequences of the decisions that you make.

If you're in need of guidance because you don't know what to do,
don't look to your friends who are in the same boat as you.

Seek the counsel of adults: parents, teachers, or pastors.
Their experience and insight may help avoid disasters.

There is no dream that is out of reach. But it will come at a cost.
Be willing to put forth the sweat and tears. Don't let your dreams
   get lost.

Dare to be responsible and one who can be trusted.
Have good ethics. Be reliable and well-adjusted.

You

Father God created you in your mother's womb.
You are fearfully and wonderfully made!
He knows the number of hairs upon your head,
His love will never fade.

Be mindful of your Father's Kingdom,
You play an important role.
But how you live your life on earth
Determines what happens to your soul.

God has a plan and a purpose for you.
You're alive for a time such as this-
To bring glory to His name
And save others from the abyss.

Be the person you were created to be
according to God's purpose and plans.
Then while you struggle through the tough times in life,
He'll shield you in His loving hands.

Be excellent. Be honest. Be humble. Be You.
Bring glory to the Father in everything you do.
Don't worry about being different. That's a great thing to be!
Take pride in and make use of your creativity.

It's okay to be silly. It's okay to be alone.
Be sure to be polite and share the things you own.
Be loving and obedient. Be forgiving, too.
Don't bend under the pressure. I dare you to be you.

About the Artist

Ana F. Stone is an award-winning artist who was born and raised in California. Throughout her childhood, Ana's parents encouraged her use of imagination and creativity but were hesitant about her making a living as an artist. To appease them, Ana studied Business instead. After several years of working corporate jobs, Ana decided to pursue her true passion by returning to school and earning a Bachelor of Fine Arts degree. After reading *Dare to Be…* written by her close friend, Kendra Kaufman, Ana felt blessed by the opportunity to fulfill a lifelong dream—to illustrate a children's book. Ana believes if we are confident in ourselves despite our weaknesses, we can inspire the world.

About the Author

Having been bullied relentlessly as a child, Kendra Kaufman knows firsthand the trauma that often accompanies growing up outside the circle of acceptance. Her profound hearing loss, glasses, braces, acne, and obesity all made her a prime target for bullies seeking to display their dominance. Thankfully, Kendra grew up in a Christ-following, Bible-believing home with unconditional love and support. Her mother never pitied Kendra's circumstances. Instead, she encouraged Kendra and challenged her to rise above them…and she did!

Kendra Kaufman wrote *Dare to Be…* to pass on those lessons she learned at home—lessons of love, faith, acceptance, and forgiveness. In doing so, she hoped to encourage, challenge, and motivate children to beat the odds they face. Kendra believes that while we may not always be able to protect our children against the onslaught of evil intentions, we *can* equip them with the tools and the foundation needed to withstand the battles when they come.

CPSIA information can be obtained
at www.ICGtesting.com
Printed in the USA
BVHW052055111119
563469BV00015BA/890/P